EXCAVATING THE PAST

THE AZTEC EMPIRE

Dr Nicholas Saunders and Tony Allan

www.heinemann.co.uk/library

Visit our website to find out more information about **Heinemann Library** books.

To order:
- ☎ Phone 44 (0) 1865 888066
- 🖹 Send a fax to 44 (0) 1865 314091
- 💻 Visit the Heinemann Bookshop at www.heinemann.co.uk/library to browse our catalogue and order online.

First published in Great Britain by
Heinemann Library, Halley Court,
Jordan Hill, Oxford OX2 8EJ,
part of Harcourt Education.

Heinemann is a registered trademark of
Harcourt Education Ltd.

Editorial: Nicole Irving, Louise Galpine and
Jeremy Smith
Design: Elaine Wilkinson
Picture Research: Jeremy Smith
Production: Edward Moore

Originated by Ambassador Litho Ltd
Printed in China
by WKT Company Limited

ISBN 0 431 14241 6
08 07 06 05 04
10 9 8 7 6 5 4 3 2 1

British Library Cataloguing in Publication Data

Nicholas Saunders and Tony Allan
Aztec Empire. – (Excavating the Past)
972' .018
A full catalogue record for this book is
available from the British Library.

Acknowledgements

The publishers would like to thank the
following for permission to reproduce
photographs: Alamy p. **43** top; Ancient Art and
Architecture p. **12** centre; Art Archive pp. **5** top
and bottom, **6** top and bottom, **7** top,
9 bottom, **10** top and bottom, **11** top and
bottom, **12** top, **13** top, **14** top, **15** top and
bottom, **17** bottom, **18** bottom, **19** right, **20**
centre, **21** top, right and bottom, **22** left, **23** top
and bottom, **24** left and bottom, **25** centre,
27 bottom right, **28–29** centre, **29** top right,
31 centre, **32** left, **34–35** all, **36** top and
bottom, **37** top right, **38** top and bottom, **39**
right, **40–41** centre, **41** right and bottom, **43**
centre; Dr Michael Smith **26** top, **27** top;
Werner Forman Archive **8–9** top, **16** top, **19** left
and bottom, **25** top right, **26** bottom, **33** left
and right, **37** bottom right, **42** centre.

Cover photograph of the Pyramid of the Sun
reproduced with permission of Corbis.
The small photograph of the feathered shield
reproduced with permission of Werner
Forman Archive.

The publishers would like to thank Dr Nicholas
Saunders, at University College London, for his
assistance in the preparation of this book.

Every effort has been made to contact copyright
holders of any material reproduced in this book.
Any omissions will be rectified in subsequent
printings if notice is given to the publishers.

CONTENTS

Dates BC and AD

BC after a date means before the birth of Christ. The years count down to 0, the date that has been taken as the year when Jesus Christ was born.

AD before a date stands for the Latin *anno domini* ('the year of the lord'). It means that the date is counted from after Christ's birth in the year 0.

Any words appearing in the text in bold, **like this**, are explained in the Glossary.

A WORLD LOST AND FOUND

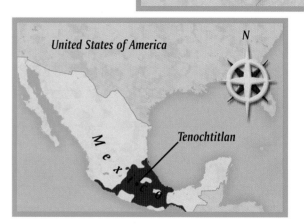

For over 3000 years the volcanic highlands and tropical rainforests of Mexico have been home to many civilizations, including the Olmecs, the Toltecs and the Maya. The most famous culture of all, however, is probably that of the Aztecs. The Aztec empire grew, flourished and died in less than two centuries. It was the last of ancient Mexico's great civilizations, destroyed at its height by Spanish invaders led by Hernán Cortés. By AD 1519, it sprawled over 200,000 square kilometres of land and was home to at least three million people, who spoke over 20 different languages.

The Aztec homeland

The Aztecs arrived in the Valley of Mexico around AD 1300 after moving south from their homeland in northern Mexico. The Valley of Mexico was a rich and fertile place, dominated by Lake Texcoco, and surrounded by an active **volcanic** landscape. This geography and the sophisticated civilization of nearby ruined cities such as Teotihuacan inspired Aztec civilization and **mythology**. They called the area Anáhuac (land by the water's edge) and used the word altepetl (mountain of water) to describe any village or town.

△ *The map above shows the extent of the Aztec empire (coloured red) and its position in modern-day Mexico. The top map shows the area around the Aztec capital, Tenochtitlan. Lake Texcoco is shown as it exists today.*

A civilization destroyed

In 1519, Spanish soldiers known as **conquistadors** arrived in Mexico in search of treasure. The Spaniards, with their guns and metal armour, were much better armed than the Aztecs, who fought with spears and bows and arrows. By 1521 Cortés had conquered the

▷ *The Aztecs had no weapons to match the Spanish soldiers, known as conquistadors (conquerors). The Spaniards had guns, but the Aztecs had only spears, clubs, and bows and arrows.*

Aztecs and claimed their empire and the whole of Mexico for Spain. No complete or undamaged Aztec monuments have survived in what is now Mexico City because the Spanish destroyed the city during the **siege** of 1521. The Spaniards looted and destroyed the Aztec capital of Tenochtitlan, and then built their new city, Mexico City, over the ruins. The speed of this rebuilding meant there was no time to destroy temple foundations or the many large stone **sculptures**. These were simply covered with rubble and built upon, preserved for future generations of archaeologists to discover.

The rediscovery of the Aztecs

The new rulers had no interest in the **pagan** Aztec heritage, which went against their **Christian** culture. They tried to hide or destroy its remains. From the 1700s, however, interest in Aztec culture began to develop. Scholars made collections of Aztec **artefacts**, old manuscripts were discovered and published, and new monuments unearthed in Mexico City. Throughout the 19th and 20th centuries more monuments and temples were uncovered and great advances were made in interpreting Aztec art and **glyphs**.

WHO WAS Hernán Cortés?

Hernán Cortés (lived 1485–1547) was a Spanish soldier who, as a young man, went to seek his fortune on the Caribbean island of Hispaniola. The governor of the island put him in charge of an expedition to explore the Mexican mainland. As soon as Cortés saw the gold and other riches in Tenochtitlan he decided to conquer it. After his victory in 1521, he became governor of New Spain (Mexico). Later he set up several other, unsuccessful expeditions to explore unknown parts of America. He finally returned to Spain in 1540, where he died seven years later.

DID YOU KNOW? The Aztecs copied architecture from past cultures such as the Toltecs.

5

The birth of Aztec archaeology

First excavations

The earliest large **excavations** took place in the 1790s in the Zocalo, the main square of Mexico City. Many of the most famous monuments were found in these early excavations, including the Coatlicue statue and the Stone of the Sun. During the 1800s, further discoveries were made by chance when foundations needed to be dug for new buildings. They included a sculpture of the goddess Coyolxauhqui, unearthed in 1825.

△ *The excavation site of the Great Temple (Templo Mayor), Mexico City. Excavations lasted from 1978 to 1982, and many exciting objects were found, including a gruesome skull rack.*

△ *This gold pendant shows Mictlantecuhtle, the lord of the dead, who was believed to rule the hells beneath the earth. It was found at the Great Temple site in Mexico City.*

Into the 20th century

The first planned excavation in Mexico took place in 1913 after workmen demolishing a building uncovered the southwest corner of the Great Temple in Mexico City. Further excavations continued around its base through the 1960s. During the 1970s, **archaeology** in Mexico City became more organized. Several projects began to excavate areas of Tenochtitlan. Then, a lucky find by workers digging a pit for power supplies led to the discovery of the Coyolxauhqui Stone at the base of the Great Temple. The site was thought to be so important that in 1978, the President of Mexico issued an order authorizing its excavation. Since then, so many discoveries have been made there that the Museum of the Great Temple was opened in 1987 to display them.

▷ *The Mesoamerican Gallery in the National Museum of Anthropology, Mexico City. This museum houses such major finds as the Stone of the Sun and the Stone of Tizoc. Treasures from other ancient Mexican cultures are also here.*

WHO WAS William H. Prescott?

William H. Prescott (lived 1796–1859), an American historian, was the man who did most to inform people about the Aztecs. He finished writing his book entitled History of the Conquest of Mexico in 1843. As exciting as an adventure story, the book was an instant success. People still read it today to learn about the Aztecs and the Spanish soldiers who conquered them.

The quest goes on

As the Aztec civilization lasted for such a short period (about two hundred years), it did not leave many monuments. In addition, many of the great temples and palaces the Aztecs built were destroyed by the Spanish conquerors. Archaeologists investigating the Aztecs concentrate on smaller sites, digging up houses to find out how ordinary people lived. These excavations have produced many everyday objects such as knives made of dark glass called obsidian, bronze sewing needles and stone mortars for grinding maize.

Archaeology Challenge

The Aztec writing system used several kinds of **glyphs**. Pictograms showed an object by its picture; ideograms expressed an idea, such as footprints to mean travel; and other signs were used where the sound of one word was similar to the sound of a different word, and could be used to express it. To read or write Aztec glyphs and make connections between sounds required a lot of knowledge and practice.

LISTENING TO THE AZTECS

One of the most valuable sources available to historians and **archaeologists** studying the Aztecs are the accounts written by their Spanish conquerors. There are also accounts called **chronicles**, written by **monks** who travelled from Spain to teach **Christianity** to the Aztecs. Finally, there are texts called **codices** by the Aztecs themselves and their neighbours of the time, which help us to imagine what life would have been like in the Aztec Empire.

△ *This is a painting of the friar Bernardino de Sahagún. His writings about the Aztecs were unread for hundreds of years, because the authorities wanted to suppress all knowledge of the Aztecs.*

Accounts from the front line

The Spanish **conquistador** and chronicler Bernal Díaz del Castillo had served in the **New World** under various commanders before joining Hernán Cortés in 1519 to help conquer Mexico. His huge work, *The True History of the Conquest of New Spain*, was written when he was an old man living in Guatemala in Central America. It tells of Díaz's experiences as a soldier serving Cortés, and describes life as a common soldier and the people he met in Mexico.

During his time in Spain, Hernán Cortés wrote five letters to the King of Spain. They provide a first-person account of the conquest of Mexico. The letters also describe his problems with creating a government, trying to get recognition for his achievements from the King and Queen of Spain, and struggling to keep his power and influence. Cortés' later letters became bitter and arrogant as eventually he lost all his power.

△ *Aztec codices (picture books) had no covers but were protected by a wooden board at each end.*

Aztec books and famous friars

Bernardino de Sahagún (1500–90) was a Spanish monk who worked in Mexico as a Christian **missionary**. He persuaded some surviving Aztecs to help produce a book of picture writing, a codex called *The General History of the Things of New Spain* (often known as the *Codex Florentine*). The **friar** Diego Durán spent his childhood in Mexico and learnt much about Aztec culture. His *Book of the Gods and Rites* and *Historia de la Nueva España* provide the most complete account of the people of the region.

Codex Florentine

This codex was compiled by Bernardino de Sahagún in the late 16th century. He spoke with old men and had them draw in the traditional way. The book has information on daily life, rituals, health and myths. This illustration shows an Aztec woman suffering from smallpox, a disease brought by a Spanish slave.

Archaeology Challenge

There are many different kinds of codices, each dealing in its own particular way with various aspects of life in ancient Mexico. They seem to offer straightforward accounts of religion, everyday life, and the Spanish conquest, but in reality they are not easy to understand. Each codex has its own problems of **bias** in terms of who made it, when and why? Finding hidden meanings, allowing for Spanish **prejudices** and Aztec ideas of history, as well as the problem of translating **Nahuatl** into Spanish, means each codex must be carefully analysed if it is to be used accurately.

A wealth of information

The codices

The Aztecs and their predecessors 'wrote' about their history, religion and day-to-day affairs using a picture-based language called pictographs. Scribes or priests drew the pictographs in books called codices (plural of **codex**). The Spaniards burnt most of the codices, viewing them as against Christianity, but some have survived. Most codices contain paintings of religious ceremonies, gods and kings, rather than everyday life, although the Codex Mendoza is an exception.

Key codices

No true Aztec codex has survived from pre-Spanish times. What we have today are codices produced by the neighbours of the Aztecs, such as the **Mixtecs**, and others painted by Aztecs after the conquest under the direction of Spanish priests like Bernardino de Sahagún. Most contain pictures with Spanish captions, though some are mainly written accounts. During the early years of Spanish rule, local communities produced documents in native style called lienzos. They often included maps of their villages and were used in their dealings with the Spanish.

Codex Mendoza

The Codex Mendoza is a collection of Aztec pictures revealing Aztec customs and history. It was painted soon after the Spanish conquest, on the order of the first Viceroy of New Spain (Mexico) to be sent to the King of Spain, Charles V. To help the king to understand it, a Spanish priest who had learned the Aztec language wrote explanations in Spanish by each picture. This page from the Codex Mendoza shows the tribute (tax) to be paid by a particular city to Tenochtitlan. It includes clothing, jewellery and a warrior's equipment.

Fragile evidence

The case of the Codex Borgia illustrates how easily codices could be damaged over time. Also known as the Book of Prophecies, Cardinal Stefano Borgia, a collector of **pagan** and Christian artefacts, found it in the hands of children, who had set it on fire. Unfortunately, the Cardinal was not able to rescue the first and last pages of the codex. On his deathbed in 1804, he gave it to the Catholic church. Today, the Codex Borgia is held in the Vatican Library, in Rome.

Codex Magliabecchiano

The Codex Magliabecchiano was illustrated for the scholar Dr Cervantes de Salazar around 1553. It has sections on the ancient calendar, monthly feasts and other festivals. The page above shows the 'Pulque Feast', with women serving maguey root beer. The Codex Magliabecchiano has fine drawings, along with a short Spanish commentary. It is one of the main sources in understanding the Aztec's monthly festivals.

Codex Borbonicus

The Codex Borbonicus was made in Tenochtitlan, probably soon after the conquest, and contains spaces meant for comments by the Spanish. It tells the reader about how the Aztec world was created, and about the Aztec gods. This page shows the god Xipe Totec and his feathered serpant Quetzalcoatl, surrounded by **glyphs** of Aztec calendar symbols. The Codex also shows the important 'New Fire Ceremony' that occurred every 52 years.

△ *Building Tenochtitlan, from the* Historia de los Indios *by Diego Duran.*

T he Aztec capital of Tenochtitlan lies today beneath the streets of modern Mexico City. Whenever building work takes place, traces of the Aztec city re-emerge. Temples, painted platforms and statues of gods have all been discovered in recent years. During the early 1960s, the pyramid-temple at Tlatelolco with its twin stairways was **excavated**, and in 1967 **archaeologists** discovered and restored a circular temple to Quetzalcoatl.

Founding Tenochtitlan

The first page of the Codex Mendoza shows an eagle perched on a cactus growing from a stone. The book tells how this had been foreseen

△ *An artist's reconstruction of part of Tenochtitlan. The Great Temple is in the centre.*

in a vision by the Aztec god Huitzilopochtli as the place where the Aztec city should be built. The Aztecs called it Tenochtitlan. The Codex Mendoza's opening page also shows the four quarters into which the city was divided. By measuring the positions of buildings and examining 16th-century Spanish maps, archeologists have shown that Tenochtitlan was built on a grid plan aligned to the gods' position in the sky. The east-west line was considered the most important because it tracked the path of the sun god Tonatiuh each day. Excavations beneath the cathedral during the 1970s revealed the remains of the Temple of the Sun God, the circular Temple to Quetzalcoatl, and the foundations of the great skull rack (tzompantli).

EYEWITNESS

'Proud of itself is the city of Tenochtitlan. This is your glory, O Giver of Life.'

15th century Aztec poem

A city of canals

The city's layout included roads and a system of canals that linked all parts of the capital. The first page of the Codex Mendoza shows four blue crossed bands, representing the canal system.

▲ *A modern painting of Tenochtitlan from the Museo Ciudad Mexico.*

Canoe transport was common, and the Spanish commented on how crowded the surrounding lake was. Knowledge of water control enabled the Aztecs to build dams, keeping fresh and salty water apart. Part of a giant **aqueduct** built to bring drinking water from the mainland has been reconstructed in the centre of Mexico City.

Archaeology Challenge

Somewhere beneath the streets of downtown Mexico City lies one, possibly two, great **ball courts** of Aztec Tenochtitlan. A plan of the Great Temple in the Florentine Codex shows shows the 'L'-shaped structure near to the skull rack, but archaeologists have not yet located it. According to the Codex Magliabecchiano the **ball game** is played with two players representing the two teams, a rubber ball, and two hoops set high into the side walls.

Written evidence

We have a number of descriptions of Tenochtitlan set down by Cortés himself in his letters to the King of Spain. In the second letter he describes his first encounter with the city of Tenochtitlan: 'After half a mile we arrived at the great city of Tenochtitlan which is situated at its centre. We met with three cities all containing very fine buildings and towers, especially the houses of the chief men and the... little temples in which they keep their idols.'

City life

Tenochtitlan was a huge city, home to a dazzling array of craftsmen, artisans, traders and priests, as well as the Aztec royal family and their servants. The city was an **imperial** capital in whose markets and storehouses could be found every kind of plant, animal and mineral from across Mexico and beyond. The Codex Mendoza illustrates the wealth of items demanded as tribute (tax) from the 450 cities ruled by Aztecs. These included different kinds of cloth, animals and skins, birds (and their plumage), tortoise shells, **jade**, and reed mats, as well as maize, honey, amber and gold. Trade was what kept Tenochtitlan alive. It took place in marketplaces across the capital, but was dominated by the huge market at Tlatelolco.

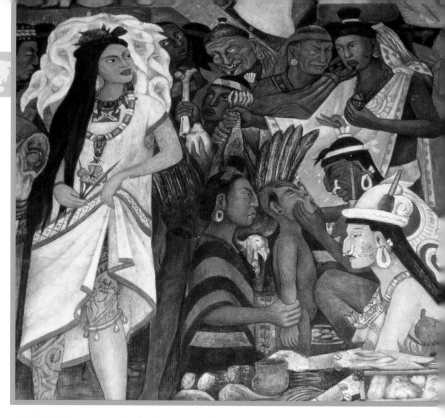

△ *This 20th-century painting by Mexican artist Diego Rivera of the busy market in Tenochtitlan is based on descriptions by Spanish soldiers.*

City living

Spanish chronicles include detailed descriptions of the Aztec capital and reveal their astonishment about what they saw there. At the heart of the city was the great ceremonial square with the Great Temple and other important buildings. Ordinary people lived in white, flat-roofed houses a single storey high; it was a crime for anyone but nobles to have two storeys or more. Wealthy citizens lived in bigger houses hidden behind windowless walls. Inside, the rooms opened out onto a central courtyard, often with a pond and gardens of brightly coloured flowers.

EYEWITNESS

'...given the choice between going to market and going to heaven, the normal Aztec housewife chose heaven, but asked if she could go to the market first!'

Account from a Spanish priest, c.1522

Tlatelolco market

Everyday some 25,000 people thronged the marketplace, and every fifth day a special market attracted 50,000 people. Spaniards who saw it were amazed at its size and the quantity and variety of its goods. The **conquistador** Bernal Díaz del Castillo describes walking amongst sellers of cacao beans, goldsmiths, and dealers in tobacco, tree-bark paper, salt and slaves. The market even had its own group of judges who maintained fair play in business transactions.

Craftsmen

Tenochtitlan had a wide variety of specialist craftsmen. Feather-working was a special skill, used to make cloaks and costumes for warriors and nobles. Moctezuma II owned a famous headdress made from shimmering green feathers, which he gave to Cortés as a gift in AD 1519. Stonemasons carved statues of the gods, metalsmiths made gold jewellery, and other workers produced sharp blades for tools and sacrifices, as well as brightly polished mirrors.

Cacao beans for money

Money did grow on trees in Aztec Mexico! In 1536, a Spanish priest called Father Motolinía wrote that cacao beans (cacahuatl) served as money as well as being the main source of chocolate. Spanish conquistadors observed how an obsidian blade cost 5 cacao beans, a turkey 100 beans, and a jade necklace 60,000 beans. Like all **currencies**, cacao bean money could be copied illegally. In the 1550s, a Spanish official called Oviedo noted that cacao shells were emptied and re-filled with earth.

DID YOU KNOW? The Aztecs called craftsmen tolteca, in honour of the Toltec civilization.

15

RELIGION AND SACRIFICE

▲ *The Coyolxauhqui Stone was found at the Great Temple site in 1978. It shows the body of Coyolxauhqui, the moon goddess, and sister of the god Huitzilopochtli.*

In 1978, workmen in downtown Mexico City accidentally dug up a great stone disk carved with the image of the Aztec Moon goddess Coyolxauhqui. It had been placed at the foot of one of the staircases of the Great Temple. **Archaeologists** then dug below the square and found the tzompantli (skull rack) outside the Great Temple. In total, archaeologists spent five years excavating the remains of seven temples. They discovered 78 buildings and an array of incredible finds, including statues and offerings to the gods.

The Great Temple

The Great Temple was a stepped pyramid, called a teocalli (god house) in the **codices**. Work began on it in AD 1325, and the temple was built in line with two sacred volcanoes nearby. On its **summit** were **shrines** to the rain god Tlaloc and the war god Huitzilopochtli. It was here that human sacrifices took place, acting out the events shown in the codices. The Great Temple contained the most important group of religious buildings in the Aztec capital of Tenochtitlan. The Spanish regarded the frightening images of gods and the bloody sacrifices that honoured them as devil worship. Beginning in AD 1525, they forced the Aztecs to pull down the temple. The speed of the rebuilding meant there was no time to remove the lower sections of the Great Temple. This meant that they were built over and accidentally preserved for almost 500 years.

shrines to Tlaloc and Huitzilopochtli

sacrificial altar

Coyolxauhqui Stone

▲ An artist's reconstruction of the Great Temple.

Burials and offerings

At the Temple, archaeologists found 100 burials full of offerings to the gods. Some contained human remains such as skulls decorated with shell and turquoise pierced by **flint** knives. Many burials contained beautifully painted pottery and stone sculptures dedicated to Tlaloc. Their green and blue colours were meant to reflect the god's mastery of rain, water and fertility. The tzompantli, showing 240 human skulls carved in stone, was one of the most gruesome discoveries. The top of the altar probably once held the heads of sacrificial victims. Animal sacrifice was also important in Aztec society. Other finds included complete skeletons of jaguars with green **jade** balls in their fangs, pumas, or crocodiles surrounded by seashells and jade.

EYEWITNESS

'There are, in all districts of this great city, many temples or houses for their idols. They are all very beautiful buildings.... Amongst these temples there is one, the principal one, whose great size and magnificence no human tongue can describe...'

Letter written by Hernán Cortés, the Spanish military leader

▲ The tzompantli (skull altar), at the Great Temple, in Mexico City.

The Aztec gods

The Aztec world was alive with powerful gods and the spirits of the **ancestors**. Paintings of them adorned the walls of the Great Temple, and filled the pages of the **codices**. Aztec gods represented different aspects of life. One example is Xipe Totec, god of springtime, who wore the skin of a victim sacrificed in his honour. As the skin dried and fell away, the Aztecs believed it encouraged the newborn corn cob to burst forth from its crinkled leaves. However, Xipe Totec also had the power to send people diseases, if they offended him. Other gods and goddesses included Chicomecoatl and Xilonen, who were often shown wearing corn cobs. They represented growth and fertility.

Huitzilopochtli

Huitzilopochtli was the Aztec tribal war god, a warrior armed with a magical weapon known as the 'fire serpent' (xiuhcoatl). The Codex Mendoza tells how he guided the Aztecs to Lake Texcoco where they founded their city of Tenochtitlan, and honoured him as the sun through war and human sacrifice. Huitzilopochtli's name means 'Hummingbird of the South', and refers to the souls of fallen warriors whom Aztecs believed were transformed into hummingbirds.

Gods of the elements

There were also gods that represented the powerful forces of nature. They appeared as supernatural characters in the codices, shaping the world through epic battles, and giving life to every feature of the earth and heavens. There were gods of wind, fire, and water, of childbirth, disease, and misfortune, as well as of the sun, moon and stars. There were two special gods in Aztec religion – the sun god Huitzilopochtli, and the rain god Tlaloc. Each was worshipped in his own **shrine** on the summit of the Great Temple.

Coyolxauhqui

The Aztecs believed Coyolxauhqui, goddess of the Moon or the Milky Way, was the evil sister of Huitzilopochtli. When she discovered her brother was about to be born she murdered her mother Coatlicue. She failed to prevent the birth, and in revenge, Huitzilopochtli killed her and **dismembered** her body at the sacred hill of Coatepec. This horrible scene was carved on a huge stone disk at the base of the Great Temple.

Tezcatlipoca and Quetzalcoatl

Tezcatlipoca was the most powerful Aztec god. Master of sorcery and human sacrifice, he saw everything through his magic mirror. He inspired such fear that the Aztecs described themselves as his slaves. Quetzalcoatl, the 'Feathered Serpent', was a benevolent god of learning, twins, and inventor of the calendar. He often appears disguised as Ehecatl, the wind god.

Tlaloc

Tlaloc represented water and fertility. Together with his assistants, the tlaloques, he sent the rains and made the crops and flowers grow. His paradise of Tlalocan shimmered with sunlight, jewels, and rich vegetation, and was the final resting place of the disabled, those killed by lightning, and those who had drowned.

DID YOU KNOW? Coyolxauhqui's story explains why bodies were thrown down temple steps after sacrifice.

Sacrifice

Sacrifice lay at the heart of Aztec religion and society. The act of sacrifice, whether human or animal, was seen as the continual repayment of the debt humans owed to the gods. Pyramid-temples and **shrines** at which gods were worshipped through acts of ritual death were found across the capital.

Aztec priests

Spanish priests recorded the activities of their Aztec counterparts in order to understand, then destroy, Aztec religion. They described Aztec priests as the guardians of sacrificial bloodletting rituals. Every night they pierced their bodies, then pulled reeds through the holes. Spanish priests also commented on the smelly and blood-soaked clothes these priests wore.

Self-sacrifice and victims

The gods Quetzalcoatl and Tezcatlipoca are shown in art and **mythology** piercing their bodies to draw blood. **Codices** and sculptures show people piercing every part of their body, though usually the tongue, ears, legs and arms, collecting the blood in a dish and then burning it. Human sacrifices were the ultimate and most valuable acts of worship. So important were they that victims were regarded not as unworthy humans, but rather as 'god impersonators'. They were groomed for their eventual death in order to please the gods.

▲ This statue of Coatlicue shows the goddess dressed in a skirt of writhing snakes, with huge animal claws for hands and feet, and a necklace of severed hands and hearts and a human skull.

◁ *This beautiful turquoise mask had a sinister purpose. It was used in sacrificial ceremonies, and the person who wore it was probably killed and eaten.*

Sacrificial tools

Knives were used to cut out human hearts and **dismember** bodies. These have been found in many places in downtown Mexico City. Black volcanic glass was used, and was identified with the god Tezcatlipoca, the inventor of human sacrifice. **Stingray** spines were also used, as were maguey cactus thorns. The former have been found in the Great Temple.

▷ *A flint knife probably used in sacrificial ceremonies to cut out the heart of the victim.*

Heart sacrifice

The pyramid at Santa Cecilia, and the innermost part of the Great Temple, had hot coals next to their shrines where human hearts were burnt. Heart sacrifice was regarded as repeating the myth in which Huitzilopochtli killed his sister the moon goddess Coyolxauhqui. The ritual is shown in the Codex Magliabecchiano, with priests carrying victims to the temple summit, stretching them over the sacrifice stone and cutting out their hearts.

Archaeology Challenge

It took experts almost 100 years to work out that the statue found in 1790 represented Coatlicue. They did so by comparing it with other known pictures of the goddess and noting that it shared certain common features – especially the serpent skirt. Today much more is known about the Aztec gods, making the job of identifying them much easier.

△ *The temple at Santa Cecilia, one of the best preserved Aztec buildings.*

AZTEC SOCIETY

In 1845, a plaque called the Dedication Stone was found in Mexico City. On it were the names of the emperor Ahuitzotl, his predecessor Tizoc, and the date 1487. It was made to celebrate a major renovation of the Great Temple. The date is important because from this point on, Aztec society quickly became an **imperial** civilization, with Ahuitzotl conquering 45 new towns according to the Codex Mendoza. The vast wealth in taxes that flowed into Tenochtitlan transformed Aztec society, public **rituals** became more elaborate and human sacrifices increased in number.

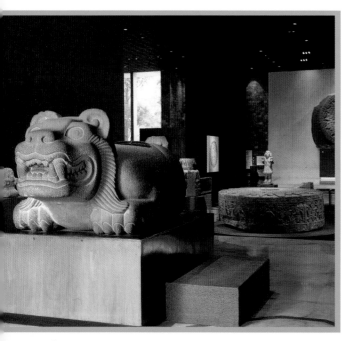

△ *This is an Aztec statue of a jaguar. In the gardens at the centre of Moctezuma II's palace, he had his own private zoo, with real pumas, jaguars, birds of prey and rattlesnakes.*

The sacred emperor

The Dedication Stone helps **archaeologists** understand how a person became emperor. The plaque shows the two emperors Ahuitzotl and Tizoc sacrificing their blood to the earth to mark Ahuitzotl's succession. The dedication of the newly refurbished Great Temple was the final ceremony in his becoming emperor.

The Florentine Codex tells archaeologists about the power an emperor had in Aztec society. It shows rulers seated on thrones covered with the skins of powerful animals such as the jaguar. This **codex** also records that during the coronation of emperors they prayed to their patron god Tezcatlipoca for guidance, and identified themselves with him. The Spanish priest Bernardino de Sahagún also records the final ceremony of the coronation involving a period of seclusion and blood offerings.

◁ *This **pictograph** from the Codex Mendoza shows Moctezuma's palace. The emperor is at the top, in the throne room. Below are meeting rooms for his generals and advisors.*

Royal palaces

Royal palaces were like small towns, with thousands of servants, courtyards, jails and storerooms. King Nezahualcoyotl of Texcoco had a summer palace at Texcotzinco where he created a terraced garden with birdcages and waterfalls, all fed by an **aqueduct**. Today, the remains form an important archaeological site, where the ritual baths, rooms and rock carvings are still visible.

Facts from the Florentine Codex

Each new emperor underwent a series of colourful rituals before beginning his reign. Dramatically staged events included the coronation itself, the new emperor fighting a Coronation War to prove his military abilities, and a final confirmation ceremony. The Florentine Codex describes the emperor making speeches to Tezcatlipoca, the patron god of royalty. The emperor asks for strength and guidance in his many sacred duties. Once crowned, he was carried on the jaguar-and-eagle throne to the Great Temple where he pierced his body with a jaguar claw in a blood offering that tied him forever to the gods.

WHO WAS Moctezuma II?

Moctezuma II (also spelt Montezuma) ruled between AD 1502 and 1520, and was emperor at the time of the Spanish conquest. Unlike the earlier Moctezuma I, Moctezuma II added little territory or tribute (taxes) to the empire, concentrating instead on holding on to previous gains. His indecisiveness when faced with Cortés and the **conquistadors** *led to his being captured and imprisoned, then killed by his own people for working with the Spanish.*

DID YOU KNOW? An Aztec emperor was considered not just a ruler but a living god.

Nobles, commoners, merchants and slaves

Aztec society was based on class. The top 10 per cent were nobles, though inheritance was less important than achieving high status through one's own actions. Several key figures helped the emperor rule the empire, and these are shown in the Codex Mendoza, seated in the Council Hall that was part of Moctezuma II's palace. The most important office was Snake Woman (Cihuacoatl). Despite the name, the position was occupied by a man.

Nobles

The Codex Mendoza shows Aztec nobles wearing their distinctive cloaks, and seated on reed thrones. Nobles paid no taxes, and were provided with an official residence from whose agricultural lands they drew their livelihood. The sons of Aztec lords were born into a junior class of nobles known as the pipiltin, from which the emperor selected many of his high officials.

△ This image from the Codex Mendoza shows a nobleman wearing a coloured cotton cloak.

The Merchants

Merchants known as **pochteca** belonged to a special class in Aztec society. A pochteca trading expedition was sometimes the first step towards war. It was also dangerous, and the gruesome death of pochteca merchants is shown in the Codex Mendoza. This stone model, found in the Great Temple, shows a pochteca carrying goods using a headstrap.

Commoners

Most Aztecs were commoners (**macehualtin**), though they could become nobles if they acted with distinction. They were organized into hereditary clans known as calpulli which themselves were divided into units of 20 families and arranged in groups of 100 households. Each calpulli had its own school and temple, and was controlled by a leader elected for life. The benefits of belonging to a calpulli were not shared by the free but landless peasants known as **mayeques**. They were either not Aztec, or had lost their rights through crime or debt.

△ *This **pictograph** from the Codex Vaticanus shows Chalchiuhtlicue, goddess of lakes and rivers, being attended by slaves. In Aztec society, slaves were often given as tribute by conquered tribes.*

The Slaves

Nobody was born into slavery, and slaves (**tlacotin**) formed perhaps only 2 per cent of the Aztec population. Although their work was unpaid, they enjoyed free food and shelter, did not pay tax, and did not serve in the army. *The Book of the Gods and Rites* has a market scene which shows traders buying and selling slaves who have large wooden collars around their necks to prevent escape. Despite this image, slaves could achieve high status, own land, and even acquire slaves of their own.

DID YOU KNOW? When nobles visited the emperor, they had to dress in plain clothes.

25

Farming, food and country life

Most evidence about Aztec life comes from the **codices** and archaeological **excavations** at the Great Temple in Mexico City. These provide information on religious **rituals** in the capital, its temples, and the life of the upper classes, but they tell us little about ordinary people in the countryside. Recent excavations at the small villages of Capilco and Cuexcomate, and the larger rural city of Yautepec, provide an exciting insight into life in the Aztec countryside.

△ *Families at Cuexcomate and Capilco lived in small one-room houses with sun-dried mud brick (adobe) walls and thatched roofs. The foundations of these houses can still be seen.*

Country life

The small farming hamlet of Capilco had 21 houses, while Cuexcomate had 150. In late Aztec times it appears that the population was growing as excavations have uncovered evidence for an increase in dam-building to water more land and produce more food. Locals were not poor. Obsidian, bronze tools, and expensive beautifully-made painted pottery have been found in almost every house. Finds of paper nearby suggest families seem to have been making bark-tree paper in their spare time, too.

The Floating Gardens

The Floating Gardens of Mexico City are the remains of a system of agriculture known as the chinampas. The Aztecs adopted this ancient system at Tenochtitlan, producing fertile garden plots by dredging the lake floor to create artificial islands separated by canals. Kept in place by willow trees, the rich soil that developed was used to grow flowers, chillis, tomatoes, maize and many other plants.

A 'rural' city

Seven Aztec houses were excavated at the Aztec city of Yautepec. They were only a little larger than those at Cuexcomate. Arts and crafts however were more developed. Plentiful evidence indicates that the population included specialist workers making blades and tools, potters making clay figurines, and other specialists involved in making cotton textiles, and also jewellery. An unexpected discovery was the royal palace of Yautepec's king which became the first Aztec palace ever to be excavated. Its courtyards, rooms, and passageway were originally covered with bright paintings.

△ *Broken pieces of ceramic cooking pots, storage jars, serving bowls and tortilla griddles give evidence for the preparation of meals by the women of Capilco and Cuexcomate.*

Food and drink

The codices tell us that Mexico was particularly rich in vegetable foods. There were no horses or cattle, and so all agriculture was done by hand. The staple food was corn cobs, ground into flour and baked as **tortillas**, or steamed as tamales stuffed with vegetables, meat and sometimes frogs. Tomatoes, chillis, rabbit, deer and turkeys were eaten, as was a hairless breed of dog. Insect eggs and water fly larvae were delicacies, and chocolate was drunk by the higher classes. The main drink was the alcoholic pulque made from the maguey cactus.

▷ *This picture from the Codex Vaticanus shows farmers harvesting maize. This was the main food in the Aztec diet.*

AZTEC TIME

In 1790, long after the Aztec civilization had been swept away by the Spanish conquest, workmen laying drains in Mexico City's main square came upon a round stone covered in mysterious carvings. It measured 1.2 metres thick, over 3 metres across, and weighed 24 tonnes. The men reported their find to the authorities, who recognized it as a monument from Aztec times. Today, this relic, known as the Stone of the Sun, is seen as one of the most important finds in Tenochtitlan and is exhibited in Mexico's National Museum. Together with the Codex Borbonicus, it casts light on the Aztec world and their view of time.

The Stone of the Sun

The Stone of the Sun is a large circular stone slab covered with intricate and once brightly-painted carvings. These designs were originally thought to represent the Aztec calendar but are now recognized as showing the five periods (or 'suns') of creation in Aztec **mythology**. The Stone of the Sun is a giant sculpture showing the history of the Aztec universe. The detail of the carving shows that the Aztecs were extremely skilled craftsmen. Today the stone is displayed in the National Museum of Anthropology, in Mexico City.

The Codex Borbonicus

The records of the 260-day religious calendar (tonalpohualli) were kept by priests in sacred books known as tonalamatl. One of the most famous examples is the Codex Borbonicus, whose pages were divided up to show brilliantly coloured paintings of the thirteen Lords of the day and nine Lords of the night. These were arranged to show their power over individual hours and days, and also over important thirteen-day weeks. The tonalamatl were magic books used by priests to predict future events and luck or misfortune in an individual's life.

▲ *An illustration showing the invention of the Aztec calendar, taken from the Codex Borbonicus.*

The two-calendar system

The Aztecs inherited a two-calendar system from earlier Mexican civilizations. The everyday calendar (xiuhpohualli) had 365 days, and was divided into 18 months of 20 days each, the extra five days being regarded as particularly unlucky. The smaller religious calendar (tonalpohualli) had 260 days, and was divided into 13 months of 20 days each. The two calendars fitted together like cog-wheels, and produced a different date every day for 52 years before starting again. This is called the 'calendar round'. At the beginning of every new 52-year period, the Aztecs celebrated the New Fire ceremony which saw the lighting of fires across the empire as a sign of renewal.

DID YOU KNOW? The Stone of the Sun used to be called the Calendar Stone.

The Stone of the Sun – close up

The Stone of the Sun's designs tell us how the Aztecs viewed time. It shows the four worlds that have ended, and the creation of the current fifth world era, thought to have been created by the Aztec gods. Aztec priests were responsible for organizing the fifth world's time into hours, days, weeks, months, and the 52-year calendar round. In the religious calendar (tonalpohualli), Aztec 'weeks' lasted 13 days, with each week controlled by such gods as Tlaloc or Quetzalcoatl. Each of the 20 days of a month was identified with a god, also shown on the Stone of the Sun. Those named after the rabbit (tochtli) were ruled by Mayahuel, goddess of the intoxicating maguey drink. Those born on rabbit days were doomed to live a miserable drunken life. For those born under the jaguar sign a glorious future as a warrior awaited them. The illustration opposite shows how the Stone of the Sun would have once looked.

Fantasy or Fact?

The Sun Stone contains a **glyph** called 13-Reed, which marks the date of creation of the fifth world era (period) by the Aztec gods. This new era or 'sun' was a renewal of the world, and so started the clock running for the sacred cycles of 52-year periods known as the calendar round. Each new 52-year period was celebrated by the New Fire ceremony. Its timing was calculated by **astronomers** who watched the movements of the group of stars known as the Pleiades. As they passed overhead, the sun rose, and a fire was sparked in the chest of a sacrificial victim. Warriors lit torches in the fire and carried them to Tenochtitlan to rekindle the temple fires. The world had been saved for another 52 years.

Day and Year Glyphs

lizard   serpent   eagle   motion

wind   rabbit   water   dog

monkey   grass   reed   ocelot

vulture   first knife   flower   death

rain   crocodile   deer   house

The signs outside the centre represent the 20 named days contained in one month. They are also used for naming years.

In the centre of the Stone is the face of the Sun God Tonatiuh, with a sacrificial flint knife for a tongue and a claw on each side. This central part of the Stone represents the fifth and current period of creation.

The Sun God is surrounded by four boxes, each containing the date of the destruction of the previous four world periods. Carved in Aztec glyphs, these earlier periods were 4-Jaguar (destroyed by jaguars); 4-Wind (destroyed by hurricanes); 4-Rain (destroyed by fire); and 4-Water (destroyed by floods).

The outer rim shows two fire serpents meeting face to face at the lower extreme. They are considered to represent the creation of the fifth world.

Archaeology Challenge

The Stone of the Sun's images and glyphs were once thought to be a combination of sundial and calendar, used to calculate the dates for religious festivals. Advances in understanding Aztec symbols led to the identification in 1921 of the central image as the Sun God Tonatiuh. The Calendar Stone was then renamed the Stone of the Sun. In 1979, new research linked the glyph dates to ordinary dates. 13-Reed commemorated not just the beginning of the fifth world period, but also relates to AD 1427, and the beginnings of the Aztec empire under the new emperor Itzcoatl.

DID YOU KNOW? During the New Fire Ceremony, Aztecs threw away everything in their houses.

31

GROWING UP AZTEC

The Codex Mendoza was written after the Spanish conquest, in 1541. Its vivid paintings in Aztec style are accompanied by Spanish descriptions which together give us a very detailed picture of everyday Aztec life, from the cradle to the grave. It takes us on an intimate journey through Aztec schools, shows us the often difficult relationships between parents and children, and describes the sometimes strange and sometimes familiar tensions and joys of getting married.

Cherished children

For the Aztecs, the birth of a child was a time of joy and danger, both physically and spiritually. The baby was delivered by a professional midwife who cut the umbilical cord and prayed to Chalchiuhtlicue, the goddess of fertility and childbirth. If the baby was a boy, its umbilical cord was given to warriors to bury on a battlefield. If it was a girl, the cord was placed beneath the hearth in the parents' home, near to the stone used for grinding corn.

◁ *A miniature mask representing the god Ixtiton. He brought children peaceful sleep.*

The Codex Mendoza describes how a newborn baby's name was chosen after the parents had consulted priests whose job it was to discover the supernatural influences associated with the time and date of the birth. If the date of birth was lucky, the baby was named the following day. If born on an unlucky day a better naming date was chosen. The name itself was announced at dawn by the midwife who had delivered the baby.

A future life

Soon after birth, baby boys were given miniature symbols of their future adult life according to their father's occupation. Some had a warrior's shield, others a goldsmith's tool, or a featherworker's knife. Baby girls were given a broom, a spindle full of cotton thread, or a basket. Once this had been done, young boys would run through the streets shouting the newborn's name and carrying a special meal of bean stew and parched corn. The Codex Mendoza tells us that boys and girls were welcomed equally into Aztec families, and were described in loving terms as 'precious necklaces' or 'beautiful feathers'.

◁ *An Aztec spear and spear thrower, miniature examples of which were given to Aztec boys.*

Archaeology Challenge

One specialist profession for which we have **archaeological** evidence is that of the paper makers. Most codices were made from native paper produced from the inner bark of the fig tree. **Excavations** at Yautepec discovered the square ridged-stones that were used to beat strips of bark fibre into flat paper. These were then trimmed to the required size, and given a chalky-white varnish onto which the scribe would draw, and then paint his images. According to the Codex Mendoza, every year saw 24,000 reams of paper paid as tax to the Aztecs.

Life for the children

Girls were educated in the home and were usually married by 15 years old. Aztec boys entered school at 15. If boys were commoners they attended the **telpochcalli**, where rules were strict. Adolescent boys learned how to build roads and repair temples but mainly they were taught the skills of war. Military training was given by experienced warriors. Boys graduated from carrying equipment for others to using their own weapons in battle.

Noble children lived in more exclusive schools known as **calmecac**. These were associated with temples, and their aim was to educate the next generation of leaders in government, the priesthood and the army. The calmecac were well stocked with **codices** that students used to learn about the gods, warfare, and **astronomical** events. Students were trained in religious matters, from sweeping temple floors to playing music for **rituals**, and by the time they left they had become fully trained warriors.

A boy's pre-school education
Education for Aztec boys before they entered school was based on teaching them skills for later life. These included fighting, but also using boats and canoes in order to work on the chinampas (floating gardens).

This disobedient son, aged 12, has been stripped naked, tied up, and thrown into a muddy puddle in the street.

This farmer is teaching his 13-year-old son to carry loads and to use a canoe.

Here, a farmer is showing his 14-year-old son how to fish.

A boy of this age would be expected to earn his keep or face harsh punishments.

A girl's pre-school education
Education for girls before the age of 15 took place at home. A girl would be taught skills that she would need to keep a home when she grew up.

▽ *The illustrations in the Codex Mendoza about bringing up children use the following key to show age and food. The red counters represent the age of the child in years, while the yellow chips illustrate the number of tortillas they were allowed to eat per day. This was an indication of the maturity of a child.*

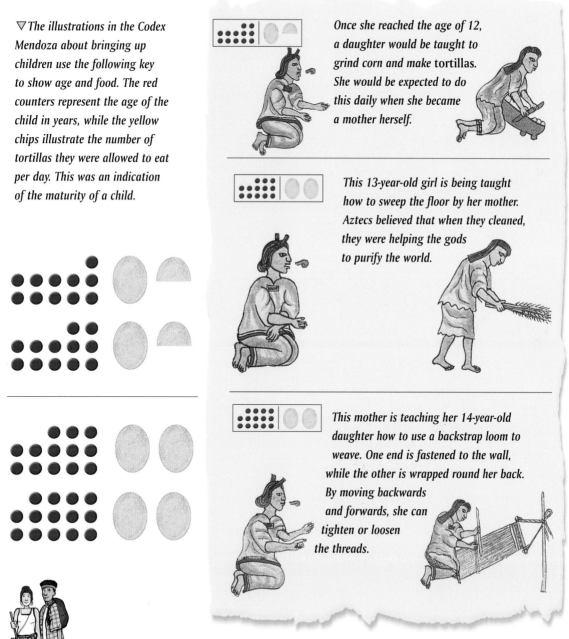

Once she reached the age of 12, a daughter would be taught to grind corn and make tortillas. She would be expected to do this daily when she became a mother herself.

This 13-year-old girl is being taught how to sweep the floor by her mother. Aztecs believed that when they cleaned, they were helping the gods to purify the world.

This mother is teaching her 14-year-old daughter how to use a backstrap loom to weave. One end is fastened to the wall, while the other is wrapped round her back. By moving backwards and forwards, she can tighten or loosen the threads.

DID YOU KNOW? Punishments for bad behaviour included being thrown into a hot fire.

Schooldays and marriage

The Codex Mendoza states young men were usually married by their early twenties, and young women by the age of 15. Parents and relatives selected a suitable bride for their son and employed an elderly woman as matchmaker. Discussions with the bride's family involved negotiations about the **dowry** paid to them by the bridegroom's family. The marriage ceremony began with feasting in the bride's house during which guests were given food, the alcoholic pulque drink, tobacco, and flowers. The bride was then carried in a torch-lit procession to her husband's house, where she sat on a reed mat with her husband and they tied their robes together. Family advice followed and several days later a final feast saw the exchange of gifts between the two families.

△ A scene from the Codex Mendoza showing training to become a warrior. The more detailed the costume, the higher the rank.

Marriage and politics

An Aztec man could have more than one wife, though he had to be able to support them. Ordinary people could usually only afford one wife, but nobles often had more. King Nezahualpilli of the city of Texcoco was said to have had 2000 wives and 144 children. In all marriages there could be only one principal wife, and she controlled all secondary wives. Political marriages between the emperor and the ruling families of other cities were a way of making diplomatic alliances.

Married life

Although women had separate roles to men, they were not considered inferior. Men were away from home for much of the year, often fighting for the emperor, and the woman was left behind to take care of the household. A man's role was to protect his wife and earn enough money to support the family. A woman was expected to be obedient to her husband. The Codex Mendoza tells us wives were told 'Obey your husband cheerfully. Do not scorn him for you will offend the goddess Xochiquetzal.'

△ An image from the Codex Mendoza, showing Aztec wives cooking at home.

Morals and divorce

The Codex Mendoza tells us that Aztec morals and behaviour were strictly controlled and punishments were severe. Divorce was possible for men and women if the marriage failed. If a wife was unable to have children or neglected her duties, or if a husband beat his wife, divorce was granted by the courts. If the husband was at fault, his wife was free to remarry, kept **custody** of any children, and was granted half of everything the couple had owned.

▷ A stone statue from the Great Temple showing an Aztec woman carrying her child and a water pot.

DID YOU KNOW? During a birth, an Aztec midwife shouted out battle cries to reflect the child fighting for life. **37**

WARFARE AND WARRIORS

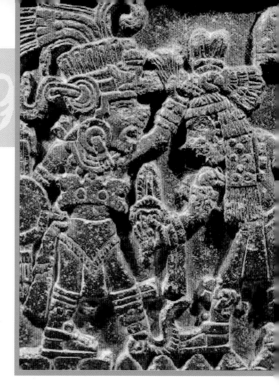

The Stone of Tizoc is a huge stone cylinder decorated with carvings of the emperor Tizoc at war. It was discovered buried near the cathedral in downtown Mexico City in December 1791. Together with the discovery of a temple outside Mexico City, statues of warriors and the evidence of the **codices**, **archaeologists** have been able to piece together Aztec beliefs about warfare.

The Stone of Tizoc

The Stone of Tizoc shows the emperor capturing the rulers of fifteen regions whose names are engraved in **glyphs** on

△ *A detail from the Stone of Tizoc.*

the Stone. Tizoc is shown grasping the hair of his opponents as a sign of his victory. The rays of the sun on the Stone's surface radiate out to the four directions of empire, reflecting the spread of Tizoc's empire. The monument was **propaganda**, as Tizoc was actually a failure as a general, and the victories commemorated here were in fact achieved before his reign began.

△ *Archaeologists think that this building in Malinalco was a ceremonial centre for Eagle and Jaguar Knights.*

The Temple at Malinalco

High in the mountains southwest of Mexico City is the temple of Malinalco, dedicated to the two elite Aztec warrior societies of the Jaguar and the Eagle. This rock-cut **shrine** has an entrance carved in the shape of a giant serpent, and at the base of the stairway stand two stone jaguar statues. Inside, there is a bench with a sculpted head of a jaguar and its paws flanked by two eagles, with a third eagle sculpture in the centre of the floor. Archaeologists think the jaguar and eagle carvings were probably the ceremonial seats of the military governors of the region.

Eagle Knights

Archaeologists digging at the Great Temple site in Mexico City found two life-size, pottery statues guarding the entry to the main room. Each one represented a man dressed in the feathers of a giant eagle, with his head peering out of the bird's open beak. By comparing these statues with illustrations from the codices, archaeologists realized that they were looking at two Eagle Knights – one of the two great Aztec military societies.

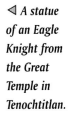

◁ *A statue of an Eagle Knight from the Great Temple in Tenochtitlan.*

Jaguar Warriors

The Codex Nuttall describes and illustrates the costumes, weapons, and tactics of warriors. Jaguar Warriors are shown wearing large jaguar-head helmets, brandishing their javelins and spearthrowers, and carrying their shields. This image is also shown in the Codex Borbonicus, where warriors are shown dressed as these animals, walking into battle. The Codex Mendoza shows several burning temples, the Aztec glyph for military conquest, and large Aztec warriors grasping the hair of smaller defeated enemies.

DID YOU KNOW? One of the reasons for going to war was to capture victims for sacrifice. **39**

Ancient Mexican war

Ways of war

The Mexican way of war was different from that practised by Europeans. The Aztecs and their neighbours waged war to impose taxes on their enemies, and to capture living prisoners for sacrifice to the gods. The key to success, as the Codex Mendoza shows, was fabulous wealth in endless lists of tribute (taxes) paid by defeated enemies, not dead bodies. A ceremonial wooden war drum from the mountain temple of Malinalco shows how much **ritual** there was in Mexican warfare. Many warriors dressed in elaborate, colourful, and impractical costumes and headdresses. For Aztec warriors who did die in battle, their souls became butterflies and hummingbirds.

Archaeology Challenge

Archaeologists think that there might be a similar temple to that of the Jaguar Warriors on the south side of the Great Temple which remains unexcavated. This is because the Aztecs created a world where everything is in balance, and also because Jaguar and Eagle Warriors played an equal role in warfare and sacrifice at the Great Temple.

Weapons

Aztec warriors wore body armour of quilted cotton, colourful costumes and headdresses. Shields decorated with feathers, mosaic or gold and turquoise inlay have also been found by archaeologists, as well as weapons including the javelin, bow, sling, and sword. The obsidian-tipped javelin was launched with a spear-thrower which added force and distance to the weapon. The Aztec sword was a long shaft of wood whose edges were inset with blades sharp enough to **decapitate** a Spaniard's horse.

A warlike society

The Codex Mendoza tells how from the age of fifteen, boys were trained as warriors and dedicated themselves to Tezcatlipoca, the master of a warrior's fate. The Codex Magliabecchiano shows a **ball court** decorated with a human skull, indicating that even public games could end in death. Public monuments such as the Stone of the Warriors, found in Mexico City in 1897, also cast light on Aztec warfare. The Stone shows the emperor Ahuitzotl and thirteen of his generals celebrating a military victory.

The War of Flowers

The War of Flowers (**xochiyaotl**) was a special type of warfare. Its name refers to the colourful costumes of warriors, and how they fell in battle like a shower of blossoms. The Codex Chimalpopoca records flowery wars between the Aztecs and the Chalca people. In the *Book of the Gods and Rites*, the Spanish priest Diego Durán describes flowery wars as designed especially to capture prisoners for sacrifice to the gods, rather than for conquest. Priests observed these battles and once they decided enough prisoners had been taken hostilities ended.

◁ *A scene from the Codex Chimalpopoca showing the Aztec War of Flowers.*

WHO WAS Moctezuma I?

Moctezuma I (ruled 1440–69) was one of the longest-lived Aztec emperors. During his rule he led the army to many victories, expanding Aztec power and forcing many cities to pay him taxes. But things did not always go well for the people under his rule. In 1450–52 a terrible drought caused many people to starve. The emperor did his best to feed them from grain stored in government warehouses.

DID YOU KNOW? Each calpulli sent a regiment of men to fight in the army.

AZTEC ARCHAEOLOGY TODAY

The investigations at the Great Temple in Mexico City were more than **archaeological excavations**. They also represented a source of pride for modern Mexicans who wished to celebrate their Aztec past as well as their Spanish heritage. Modern archaeology embraces such ideas, mixing cultural traditions with history and science to present a dazzling past to younger generations.

△ *Men dressed as jaguars re-enact a blood sacrifice to the Jaguar God.*

The Shrine of Guadeloupe

Mexican society today is a curious mix of Catholic religion and the old Aztec ways. An example of the old ways is the **Christian** cult of the Virgin of Guadeloupe at Tepeyac in northern Mexico City. Originally this area was sacred to the Aztec goddess Tonantzin who was addressed in prayers as 'Our Mother'. After the Spanish conquest, the area became Christian when a shepherd who had converted to Christianity had a vision of the Virgin Mary and built a church on that spot to honour her.

Blood for the Jaguar God

The remote mountain village of Acatlán in southwest Mexico was founded during Aztec times. Each spring, people hold a **ritual** which echoes blood sacrifices by the Aztec Jaguar Warriors. Young men dressed in jaguar costumes fight each other in pairs on the summit of a local mountain known as Blue Mountain. The fights begin in early May, and villagers believe that if they shed the powerful blood of young men, the Jaguar God will be pleased and send the rains to fertilize the corn crop.

▷ *A shrine, complete with skeletons and marigolds, laid out to mark the Mexican Day of the Dead, celebrated in November.*

Day of the Dead

Another example of the mixing of the old and new is the Day of the Dead or All Saints Day celebrations that take place annually in early November. Before the Spanish conquest, skulls and skeletons featured in Aztec art partly to frighten and intimidate their enemies. Today miniatures of these are made of sugar and chocolate as sweets for children. Families spend the night at the graves of their relatives that they adorn with brightly coloured flowers – a typically Aztec touch. As did the Aztecs, many modern Mexicans believe that if you don't honour the dead in this way they return to haunt you.

◁ *Mexico's highest mountain, Pico de Orizaba, was the site of an Aztec shrine, found in 2001.*

New finds

In 2001, a stone Aztec **shrine** dating from the 15th century was found some 4260 metres up the 5480 metre-high Pico de Orizaba, Mexico's highest mountain. It may have been built to honour the rain god Tlaloc. It is in a line with two nearby peaks, La Malinche and Cerro Tlaloc, suggesting it was also used by the Aztecs to watch the stars.

Archaeology Challenge

For information about the details of daily life in ancient times, archaeologists often rely on middens – ancient rubbish dumps. By searching through the household waste of past times they can learn a surprising amount about how people lived, the work they did around the house, the food they ate and the vessels they prepared it in. The study of some Aztec middens has unearthed not only thousands of fragments of broken cooking pots and storage jars, but also many tiny clay figurines, thought to have been used in household religious rituals.

For the early part of their history the Aztecs were a nomadic tribe that wandered up and down the Valley of Mexico, seeking land in which to settle. In 1325, they finally found an island on Lake Texcoco and by 1350 had built Tenochtitlan, which was to become the centre of their empire. The Aztec civilization lasted just over a century longer, before the Spaniards took their country from them in 1521.

AD

c.1100–1200 AD
The Aztecs leave their original home in the wilds of northern Mexico in search of a better home with more land.

c.1300
The Aztecs arrive in the Valley of Mexico as a small, hungry band of homeless wanderers.

1325
The Aztecs settle on a small island near the shore of Lake Texcoco, where they will build their future capital, Tenochtitlan.

c.1350
By this time the Aztecs are one of about 20 different tribes all struggling for power in the Valley of Mexico.

1376
Acamapichtli, a member of the ruling family of the neighbouring city-state of Culhuacan, becomes Aztec ruler. He is the first Aztec leader whose name is still known today.

1426
The Aztec ruler Chimalpopoca is killed on the orders of the king of the powerful neighbouring city-state of Azcapotzalco.

1427
The new Aztec king, Itzcoatl, makes a Triple Alliance with two other nearby city-states to take revenge on Azcapotzalco.

1428
The Aztecs and their allies conquer Azcapotzalco, destroying the city. They then become the chief powers in the Valley of Mexico.

1440
Moctezuma I, the greatest Aztec emperor, comes to the throne.

1450–52
A terrible drought strikes the Aztec lands, leaving thousands of people dead.

1473
The Aztecs conquer the neighbouring island of Tlatelolco in Lake Texcoco, and join it by a causeway to their capital of Tenochtitlan. The capital's main marketplace will grow up there.

1487
The Great Temple in Tenochtitlan is rebuilt bigger than ever. Over 20,000 human victims are sacrificed in a four-day ceremony when it is completed.

1502–20
Moctezuma II becomes the last Aztec emperor.

1519
Spanish conquistadors led by Hernán Cortés arrive on the coast of Mexico.

1520
Moctezuma II invites Cortés and his soldiers to stay as guests in his palace. They respond by taking him prisoner. He is finally killed by his own people when he makes a speech telling them not to resist the Spaniards, who are then driven out of the city.

1521
Cortés returns with more troops and besieges the city. It falls after a 93-day siege. The Spaniards enter in triumph and take control of the whole Aztec empire.

1535
Mexico becomes a colony of Spain.

1547
Hernán Cortés dies in Spain.

1567
Cortés' body is brought back to Mexico and is buried in the cathedral built using the stones from the Aztec's Great Temple.

TIMELINE OF AZTEC ARCHAEOLOGY

1520s

The Spanish conquistador Hernán Cortés writes several letters back to the King of Spain about his experiences in Aztec Mexico.

1540s

The Spanish viceroy Antonio de Mendoza commissions the Codex Mendoza to capture Aztec culture for the King of Spain.

The Friar Bernardino de Sahagún compiles a book called the Florentine Codex: General History of the Things of New Spain on Aztec history, customs and religion.

1570s

The Spanish conquistador Bernal Díaz del Castillo's account of what he had witnessed during the conquest, *The True History of the Conquest of New Spain,* is published in Spain.

1790

Workmen building drains in the centre of Mexico City discover a huge statue of the Aztec goddess Coatlicue. The statue is later reburied because Spanish priests consider it 'devilish'.

1791

Workers employed on the same job make two other important discoveries, both of carved circular stones weighing many tons. One will become known as the Calendar Stone, the other as the Stone of Tizoc.

1821

Mexico wins independence from Spain, making it easier for foreign archaeologists to visit the country.

1823

The statue of Coatlicue is dug up again and put in a museum.

1884

The Mexican archaeologist Leopoldo Batres starts to excavate the ancient city of Teotihuacan, which flourished in the Valley of Mexico 1,000 years before the Aztecs arrived.

1900

Further Aztec finds are made when new sewers are laid in Mexico City.

1964

The National Museum of Anthropology opens in Mexico City to house the world's best collection of Aztec treasures.

1966

Construction of a new underground railway system begins in Mexico City. Many Aztec artefacts are discovered.

1967

The temple of Ehecatl-Quetzalcoatl is discovered when the Pino Suarez metro station is built.

1978

Workmen laying electrical cables in the centre of Mexico City discover the Stone of Coyolxauhqui, another important Aztec relic.

1978–82

Following the workmen's find, a major archaeological project gets under way to excavate the remains of the Aztec Great Temple and surrounding buildings.

1988

The Stone of Moctezuma I is unearthed from the gardens of the Archbishop's Palace in Mexico City.

1992

Over 200 precious metal bars are recovered from a shipwreck off Grand Bahama in the West Indies. The bars are thought to be Aztec gold, silver and copper plundered by the Spaniards and melted down. Archaeologists date the bars to between 1521–35 – around the time when the Aztec empire collapsed.

2001

Archaeologists discover a stone Aztec shrine on the Pico de Orizaba mountain in Mexico. Built to honour the rain god Tlaloc, it dates from the 15th century.

2002

Remains of Aztec city found under the 18th century Chapultepec castle by archaeologists - the first time parts of the city have been found in the suburbs of modern Mexico City. Archaeologists discovered fragments of ceramics, figurines of deities and needles made of bones used for needlework.

GLOSSARY

ancestors

Persons from whom somebody is descended.

aqueduct

A pipe or channel designed to carry water.

archaeology

The scientific excavation and study of the remains of past societies, such as buildings, dead bodies, tools and pottery.

artefact

An object made by people, such as a tool or an ornament.

astronomy/astronomical

The scientific study of the stars, planets and other bodies that make up the universe.

ball court

Area of ground on which a ball game is played.

ball game

A game played in Central America in which players tried to knock a rubber ball through hoops without using their feet or hands.

bias

A leaning towards a particular viewpoint.

calmecac

School for the children of nobles.

Christian

Person who follows Christian religion, believing Jesus Christ is the Son of God.

chronicle

A register of events, often in the order in which they happened.

Codex (plural - Codices)

A book or books filled with a picture-based language called pictographs.

conquistador

Spanish word for 'conqueror', describing the Spanish soldiers who conquered much of Central and South America in the 1500s.

currency

A type of money particular to a country.

custody

To care for or guard somebody.

decapitate

To slice the head off someone.

dismember

To cut into pieces.

dowry

Property or money given to a bride by a bridegroom's family.

excavate/excavation

The process by which archaeologists dig up ground when looking for artefacts.

flint

A hard stone flaked to form a primitive tool or weapon.

friar

A member of certain special orders of Christian monks who go out to preach their message in public.

glyph

A carved character or symbol.

imperial

Something characteristic of an empire.

inscription

In archaeology, an historical or religious record that is carved, painted or written on a hard surface such as stone or metal.

jade

A precious green stone, used to make jewellery and statues.

macehualtin

The name of an Aztec commoner.

matchmaker

Someone paid to arrange a marriage.

Mayeques

Landless but free peasants.

missionary

Somebody who tries to convert another person to their religion.

Mixtec

A culture of southern Mexico that existed just before the Aztecs.

monk

Someone belonging to one of various Christian religious orders.

mythology

A collection of stories associated with a particular culture.

Nahuatl

The official language of the Aztecs, still spoken today.

New World

North and South America.

pagan

A person or thing not identified with any of the main religions.

pictographic

Writing that uses pictures rather than letters; so, a picture of a house means 'house'.

plaza

An open square in the centre of a town or city.

pochteca

A name given to Aztec merchants, who had special rights and privileges in society.

prejudice

An opinion formed without examination of the facts.

propaganda

Material spread to support a cause.

ritual

The special words and actions of a religious service or ceremony.

sculpture

To work a material such as stone into a three-dimensional figure.

shrine

For the Aztecs, a small building sacred to a god, often set on top of a stepped pyramid.

siege

The surrounding and blockading of a city in an attempt to capture it.

skull rack

Rack to display the skulls of sacrificial victims.

stingray

A poisonous fish.

summit

The highest point of something.

telpochcalli

A school for Aztec commoners.

tlacotin

The Aztec name for a slave.

tortilla

A thin Mexican cake or bread.

volcanic

Something related to volcanoes.

xochiyaotl

The Aztec name for a special type of war called the War of Flowers. Warriors fought to show their skill and take captives for sacrifice rather than killing each other.

FURTHER READING

U.K.

Avoid Becoming an Aztec Sacrifice!,
Fiona MacDonald
(Book House, 2002)

The Land of the Five Suns: Looking at Aztec Myths and Legends,
Kay McManus
(British Museum Press, 1996)

U.S.

The Aztec News,
Scott Steedman
(Candlewick Press, 2000)

The Sad Night: The Story of an Aztec Victory and a Spanish Loss,
Sally Schofer Mathews
(Clarion, 1994)

U.S. AND U.K.

Growing Up in Aztec Times,
Marion Wood
(US Edition: Troll, 1993.
UK Edition: Eagle Books, 1993)

How Would You Survive as an Aztec?,
Fiona MacDonald
(US Edition: Orchard Books, 1997.
UK Edition: Franklin Watts, 1994)

INDEX

Titles in the *Excavating the Past* series include:

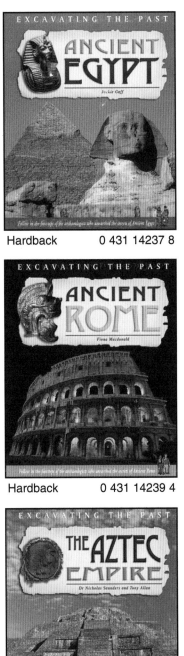

Hardback   0 431 14237 8

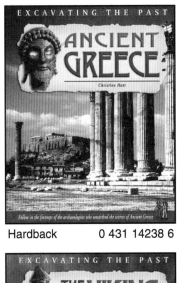

Hardback   0 431 14238 6

Hardback   0 431 14239 4

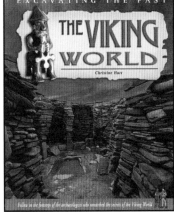

Hardback   0 431 14240 8

Hardback   0 431 14241 6

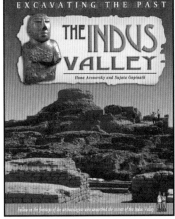

Hardback   0 431 14242 4

Find out about the other Heinemann Library titles on our website www.heinemann.co.uk/library